Beholdings

BEHOLDINGS

Poems by
BETTY ADCOCK

Louisiana State University Press
Baton Rouge and London
1988

Designer: Sylvia Loftin
Typeface: ITC Garamond
Typesetter: Focus Graphics
Printer: Thomson-Shore, Inc.
Binder: John H. Dekker & Sons

10 9 8 7 6 5 4 3 2 1

Library of Congress Cataloging-in-Publication Data
Adcock, Betty.
    Beholdings: poems/by Betty Adcock.
      p. cm.
    ISBN 0-8071-1465-0 (alk. paper). ISBN 0-8071-1466-9 (pbk.: alk.
    paper)
      I. Title.
    PS3551.D396B44 1988
    811'.54—dc19   87-33247
                                                                  CIP

Publication of this book has been supported by a grant from the National
Endowment for the Arts in Washington, D.C., a federal agency.

The author extends special thanks to the National Endowment for the
Arts for a Fellowship in Poetry, which made the writing of this book pos-
sible. Grateful acknowledgment is also made to the following publica-
tions, in which some of these poems originally appeared, sometimes in
slightly different versions: *Carolina Quarterly*, *Georgia Review*, *Helicon
Nine*, the *James Dickey Newsletter*, *Negative Capability*, *New Virginia Re-
view*, and *Tar River Poetry*. "Digression on the Nuclear Age" and "Rent
House" first appeared in *TriQuarterly*, a publication of Northwestern Uni-
versity.
    Some of the poems in Part I are based on material in articles by Alice
Cashen, Dean Tevis, and Ellen Walker, in Francis E. Abernethy (ed.), *Tales
of the Big Thicket* (University of Texas Press, 1966). Information on the
Caddo confederacy and the Ays tribe comes from the following sources:
W. W. Newcomb, Jr., *The Indians of Texas* (University of Texas Press, 1961);
John R. Swanton, *Source Material on the History and Ethnology of the
Caddo Indians*, Smithsonian Institution's Bureau of Ethnology Bulletin
No. 132 (1942); and George L. Crocket, *Two Centuries in East Texas*
(Southwest Press, 1932).

Contents

Beholdings

Clearing Out, 1974

After this kind of death, sudden and violent,
there's difference forever in the light.
Here's the sun I'll see from now on
aslant and keeping nothing
in its backward look. I have become rich
with disappearance. I have become this light

pooled now on my father's desk,
his grandfather's—rolltop sturdy as a boat
and ice-locked in a century of deepening afternoon.
I have to open it and take the cargo on
myself. There's no one else.

Forget the pigeonholes with their indifferently kept
papers waiting to fly out and be important.
They were never important, the cash and receipts,
leases, royalties, mortgages wadded here like trash.
Forget the checkbook that was awash with blood,
and the wallet, its pictures crusted dark.
Everything in his pockets was afloat.
A man shot in the stomach drowns
what's on him. Let the *personal effects*
stay in their labeled plastic sack. Go on

as if this were a forest with a path.
It's like him to have kept a jay's flightfeather,
old now to crumbling, though it holds to blue
like a blind man's memory of sky;
and a terrapin shell bleached of all camouflage,
white dome of cyclopean masonry in scale,
packed with the shape of silence as a bell;
a wild boar's intact lower jaw, the yellowed tusks
like twists of evil weather caught in sculpture,
dusty in a scatter of red cartouches,
the shotgun cartridges gone soft as cloth.

One drawer's half filled with pocketknives,
all sizes, jumble of dark hafts like a cache
of dried fish. Opened, these could still
swim through to sapling heart. To bone.

He had a good eye. With any kind of blade
he'd make a creature walk straight out of wood
into your hand. The few he didn't give away
are gathered here, votive and reliquary:

bear with her hitch-legged cub,
dove in a tree, wild turkey open-winged,
two deer with antlers slightly off
—imperfect the way antlers really are—
and a razorback, a bobcat in a leap.
And then the horses.
My mother gave him real woodcarver's knives,
cherished in their box and not once used.

The best of the figures is the bucking horse,
body like a hauled-back bow.
Even on this scale the strain, the shine
of muscle showing, wind in a flung stirrup.
And all the intricate heave of wished-for power
is drawn down to a block two inches square,
four hooves and the head locked on the moment
arching off that little ground.

Drawerful of keys, marbles, arrowheads, rocks
he saw some form in. Keys to nothing standing.
There's a grace to the thin-shanked instruments
whose ends look like dull claws, the kind old houses
had for every room; blunter keys for barn lots,
cabins that held the violated lives of slaves,
cotton houses, lawyers' offices, stores
that ran on barter.

A peace comes to this sorting.
When my grandmother was a girl, she raised a fawn.
It went wild afterward in our woods. Later,
a buck full-grown thumped up the steps one night
onto the porch outside this very window,
slipping and knocking antlers on the rail.
Framed in the lamplight for one still moment,
the strange known eyes looked in,
and the young woman looked at him.
It's the part of every story we remember,

2

the dream lost track of, changed
and coming back.

Distance has webbed my eyes like cataract,
thickening like an ice sheet I must lift.
Heavy with damp,
here is the Teal Bible, 1815,
brought to Texas with the first encampment
of Anglo settlers. It's pure living mystery
why they came. Unless that's what they came for
after all, with no way to answer
except the ways to kill; and no new dream enough
to staunch the stubborn longing to recover
what vanished in their footprints.

My great-grandfather's whistle carved of horn.

A cedar knot, deep turn in the red heart
heavy and separate. Nick it, and the scent
of cedar pours out like a sound, that thick.

Wild turkey caller whittled out of pine,
all confirmation gone.

The hunter's horn with one note for the lost.

And a perfect doll-sized real cane-bottomed
chair in a bottle.

That's the lot. I'll take what matters,
blood and documents, to the life I made elsewhere,
that place so far different in this light
you could get the bends between here and there.
The animals in wood, the stones, the silence caught
in terrapin's shell and turkey's pine voicebox,
this desk itself—a beholding full
of time before the tree was cut to build it—
I set all adrift, dismantled vessel, log raft,
rough-layered rings of association
like a language widening.
And the loosed river takes it
toward the turning sawblades of our dawn.

A Greek poet said it. Thémelis:
What would death have been without us?

3

I

In deep East Texas, we croon to each other. We sing to each other in a high lifted tone, especially in times of greeting or farewell. . . . An East Texan may touch you while talking, just a light touch on the arm or shoulder. The touch is to be sure you don't go away. He is telling you a story. East Texas talks in stories. You have to stay there until the story's done.

—from a column by Gordon Baxter
San Augustine *Rambler*

Ancestors

*The plant and animal life of the Big Thicket [of East Texas]
has led writers to refer to the area as "the biological cross-
roads of North America."*

—*Natural History* magazine
April, 1986

*I have been in the heart of the Big Thicket for ten days. Noth-
ing can be seen except the tangled underbrush and tall
trees. In a ride of 150 miles . . . there is one continuous
dense growth. As far as the eye can see it is the same; the
tangled undergrowth and fallen trees interpose an almost
impassable barrier. . . . In many places we have had to go
on our hands and knees.*

—John A. Caplen, 1887

The first immigrants spoke then with their winds,
voices of bone cold issued of moonlight and the dim
sun cool as a metal knife.
               Vaster than any herd, whiter
than the future that would stream from Europe,
these came halfway
               from where the ice is dreamed.

Like gods breathing in another sphere, making
and unmaking, they locked the sea in a tall
radiance and loosed it again, every time
building the peculiar clays and gravels
of these abrupt edges,
               this wedge of no account,
                         banking on it.

And in the ice-foot's final retreat, pure journey
released itself—the grandfather rivers poured and carrying
south as if the continent tilted like a board.
In the tongues of dissolution,
               in the descant of new winds,
in the changed-again slang
               of animal footprints,

the lissome ghosts of the great glaciers sang
downmelt, sang the no longer lonesome
airs, sang even in the wildfire-children
of the sun come back, sang buried
in earth's shifts until the mastodon was
right here; and the giant armadillo,
dire wolf and tapir and American horse
were here and gone, their bones
laid down like masonry under

        the curiously blent
and gently separating

        live crosscurrents blowing
from mountains and great plains, from tropics south,
from eastern forests and far western deserts.

And they sang
     prairie grasses of forty kinds, white prickly poppy,
hibiscus flowers eight inches across, Oklahoma clover, dog sunshade
desert lavender, silverleaf nightshade, yucca, and cactus—
   preached
      longleaf-bluestem uplands, stagger bush,
Kansas gay-feather, bottle gentian, butterwort, New Jersey tea,
Carolina lily—
   called forth
      Missouri ironweed, Virginia
buttonweed, seaside heliotrope, fringe-tree, leather flower,
Mexican big plum—
    whispered
      mayhaw, spagnum, bogmoss, dwarf
palmetto, carnivorous blossoms of four kinds, ty-vine, yaupon,
burmannia, resurrection fern, Dakota vervain—
      told understory
to oaks of fifteen kinds, hickories, sycamore, pines to 150 feet,
bald cypress, tupelo and sweet gum, black cherry, pecan,
four wild magnolias, hop-hornbeam, elm, beech, birch, planertree,
farkleberry, sugarberry, mountain laurel, ironwood, walnut, cedar,
cottonwood, willows, maple, buckeye, hawthorn, soapberry, dogwood,
wahoo, devil's-walking-stick, hollies, corkwood, the forest ongoing
multiple and shading sometimes orchids of twenty kinds, climbed by

rattan, edging to giant cane, Kentucky wisteria, strawberry, dewberry,
Arkansas blueberry—
                    and breathed Appalachia down
                                        in bloodroot,
lady's slipper, and yellow dog's tooth violet.

Only this forever unfinished, dragged-up land, its grit-gray
and red clays, quartz sands, saline outcrops, loams, acid bogs
and mima mounds—all odd proximities ridged and original,
leveed, hummocked, flattened, raised dry and let down
into baygall and bayou—only this riled ground set into weather
would be bitter and sweet enough, patchworked and strange
and changeable enough to take
                              every kind of seed and treeling
and hitchhiking gifted spore
                              to raise up and keep
in rare compacted home
                              this unlikely enisled
specifically local
                              violent green democracy

whose gifts were the bear and bobcat and black bee,
panther and deer, wolves of three kinds, fox
of the narrow shoulders, high-backed hog
with his slant attack,
                              and a silvering
of the black-fingered rivers with fish,
                                        a sky graven
with whole countries of birds whose vast
                                        migrations cross exactly
here.

And the surround was a fierce susurrous of names:
Atakapa, called by the Choctaw word for man-eater,
Karankawa, bodies smeared with alligator grease,
Patiri, Badai, Hasinai of the grass houses
and eternal temple fires, and Ays, remembered least.
Even these skirted what they called Big Woods
or went in only with the clear directions
of water, on the whisper of canoes.

9

When the white, the ice-eyed European,
by his own abstract interior cold
was driven here to stay, it was little
by little. It was on his hands and knees
for the hacked-out bad farm, a house
with a dobber chimney of mud and Spanish moss,
for the forests that could fatten hogs
and cattle without help.
At the fertile, easier northern edge,
a few log-cabin aristocrats with their slaves
seeped down from Virginia and Tennessee,
opened wide cotton fields and wore them out.

Far in deep, nothing opened easily,
and a few could live with that. And time
did bring logging trails, crews
to take the giants, to bring out turpentine,
and cash to be had from barrel staves,
from railroad ties hand-cut
to size on the spot in hell's own heat
by men wearing nothing at all but shoes and hats.

By the time the myth-drinkers from the cities
came to pay good money to be guided on bear hunts;
by the time the photograph was snapped
of the tree from which the last bear toppled;
by the time panthers and red wolves were scarce
And drill rigs had plumbed the oily sloughs
where wild hogs rolled to rid themselves of flies;
by the time the last immigrants could stand up straight
in the clear-cut heart,
they were part of a far new cold
rising tall and its shadow cast down
beyond them, a terrible singing.

Ays

I

    The name softens in the bayou,
borne on that murmur, and anchors in wrong letters
on the black bridge marker: the local mispronunciation
        Ayish—anyhow
      it goes on being gone.

    And it must have sounded, said right,
like a cry, like something between a cry and ashes,
        what wind and earth will take.
      So little
      is known of the people who spoke
themselves in it, the spell of their living,
      I think my father—
I think my father with his boyhood's hoard
of scrapers, handaxes, bowls, and arrowheads,
must have held the heavy unhearable echo
      of all that was left to know.

    From the fields at the broken foot
of our farm, from the stony rise that's still
      called Mission Hill,
he fished their village up,
hearthsites and graves blindsided lightward
      by the shovel-load and scrabble
of a boy's dream-ridden hands in 1915, imagining,
given to imagine, another kind of Indian—
      plains-eyed, horseback and dangerous.

    And when the ceremonial stones
in their perfect pairs, and the points of every size,
the pipes and awls and quick-fired shards
      were stolen in turn from him,
      in his seventieth year taken
by persons unknown, persons unknowing, who must have sold
the lot to a back-street dealer in Dallas or Houston
      where there'd be no questions about origin,

      then I think my father crying
as one might cry for kin, and not for the simple
serious forms but for unknown echoes around them,

11

something never unearthed of his own,
a firesite blackened and fine-sifted as sorrow is
when it cannot be spoken, having become the ground,
and the longing forgotten:

those magical far-eyed horses that never came.

II

From 1721 until 1773 the Zacatecan Franciscans
passed out bribes and God and smallpox
from one of Spain's more outlandish missions:
Nuestra Señora de los Delores de los Ays.
Abandoned after fifty years without a convert—
in all that time, not one—it goes on sinking
underneath that little hill beside the cow pasture.

In 1807, the Ays were said to be *extinct*
as a nation, there being only twenty-five souls.
No other Indian Nation speaks their language,
though they speak Caddo when among those tribes,
with whom they are in amity. So wrote Sibley,
an agent under Thomas Jefferson.
Today I traded a shawl to an Ays woman
in return for an alphabet. This is lost.

The eighteenth-century travelers' reports
and the few letters from the mission's priests
to the Viceroy (if we set aside the rancor
and the elaborate righteousness) present
a ragtag woodland people with a sense of humor.
Hedonists, by all accounts not violent,
they were fond of the friars' gifts of bluest cloth
because that color was the sky's,
possessed of *the richest lands in all this province*,
given to ease, trickery, festival *mitotes.*
And surprisingly given to hard argument
with any priest who spoke to them of the new God.
An exception is set forth in one report
by a padre who'd told an unintended truth
when he announced to the unconverted

that the God he preached sent pestilence.
For once, he was not disputed.

They were thought to be a fallen remnant
of a people older than the Caddo in this region:
the usual pattern, a disconnected language,
isolation, the dominant tribes' long-held opinion
that these Ays were inferior and degenerate.
Theirs is a story with not much in the way
of imagination, being only a kind of tuneless song
no one has heard, or wanted to.
It was a boreal wisp in the air above our town
and in my father's room where dust had hold
of rows of dim glass cases filled with the dislodged
handwork of the dead, that breakage
drifting always under ours.

Trying to put it together, I come upon
not much more than their small name
the sources spell a dozen ways
so there's no telling it. I come upon
the one kernel of perfect refusal,
and the fever of their whole vanishing
hardens into this:

that they missed the sorry reservations,
the circus of broken treaties, wild West
shows, dime novels, movies; missed
the scrutiny of ethnologists and moved past
the skewed, befeathered myths we would set up
anew each decade like stuffed birds.
They missed by a whole century the ruinous fervor
touched with Christian resurrection lore:
Ghost Dance rolling down from the Great Plains
to all the fenced and dying-piecemeal cultures,
raising even the docile, changed Caddo,
who'd been removed by then to Oklahoma,
to last-ditch dervishing that failed and failed.

And they are not anywhere from our final turn,
this dance we've always done in our strange will.

our love's distorting lens on what we kill.

This is a story without heroes,
its axis one exquisite fishhook of carved stone,
bone-colored, still sharp, exacting. Taken.

III

I turn from memory and books, translations,
        to speak to the boy my father
where he sits in a slice of the sun of 1915
laying out arrowheads with the dirt still on them,
        wrongheaded patterns on a Turkey rug,

        in the shape-shifting intensity of dream
that would burn for him in the forms behind glass,
be scattered at last like an alphabet unstrung,
        be nameless as ashes or money.

        My father, only this much is certain:
        it was the custom among them
to weep as a greeting to strangers. It was their custom
        to stain themselves red with the clay of this bayou.
They were known by the tribes to be less than the others,
        lazy, not dependable, not brave people.

        They were known to have the best sorcerers.

Big Thicket Settler, 1840s

Aus Hooks watched one ox list like a drunk deacon
and fall stone dead, no reason given
among hummocks and baygalls, ferns tall as the wagon,
oaks and cypresses standing higher than steeples.

Coming into the bottoms, he'd seen a world
unbraked, changeable as the roil of delirium.
Nights were swampfire, nets of mosquitoes
that never let him loose. Dawns like dough.
Rags of fog now tattering past, and the wagon

steep with household suddenly tilting
one-sided as history
with only the one beast to pull it.

Aus Hooks standing and looking:
chair leg and kettle, harness and mattock
paled in the faint rust red of wetted dust,
the wagon dampening as if a box could sweat,
trunk and plow handle fading, eaten
like meat in this light, this light

alive with the rivers in it, tides of birds
and an arkspill of animals ungatherable
in gnarling leaflight too clotted
to aim through for a shot. All, all a drowning
downfall rot of trees, vines not even God
could have wanted. Aus Hooks dropped the reins,
dropped *homestead* and *new land*, dropped
under onrushing morning like a worn-out
swimmer under white water,
losing, it might be, even his name
and striking a shoulder hard on the wagon
to remind his flesh of its separate home.

Journey unspooled itself, turning
like the movements of bad sleep on him
in this air that was not rain but smoke
from a green heat burnless. He chose
what his wife would have chosen,
Bible and tintype, and what he'd need.
Then he shot the other ox where it stood,
and he set, among the trunk's clothes, fire
to say whatever it would to the molten
unhaltable kingdom before him, some notion
of *harvest* adrift in his mind like a tune,
while the wagon turned tall as a hayrick and golden.

Had it been possible, he would have thought
a prairie, hard, dry land clean-scoured
to absence waiting to be filled
with what his kind could bring, their work,

15

their legend, their pining women;
a place that would keep inside
its clear horizon lines and leave him his,
wind and empty weather he'd come to understand
in time. But such a land was not quite yet
available to thought.

Aus Hooks walked back to Georgia, straight
as a pillar of salt.

Kaiser's Burnout

Jayhawkers, an army, and fire are the reasons
there's a prairie in the middle of these woods
a hundred and twenty years
after the last of the smoke cleared.

Warren Collins and his boys and all their cousins
thought the Union ought to stay, already put together
like it was—like a marriage or a dwelling-house—
and because whatever seam up there had split
was too far away to think about, this deep
in East Texas. You couldn't call them Jayhawkers exactly,
since not much politics was in it. They were just poor
and they had thought it out, living where a panther
could spook your woods cattle, or a bear
get at your hanging hogmeat if you didn't watch it.
They thought they wouldn't go this time to war.

And that was fine until Captain Charlie Bullock,
a man pretty nearly local, but out of Woodville,
got sent by a Galveston officer named Kaiser
to do something about it with militia.
The Collins boys heard ahead, and they lit out
for the Thicket where it's tight.
They dug two wells for water to last them
in a place still known as The Union Wells,
and brought in supplies. They'd depend on game
for the long haul. In another war, Sam Houston
had a plan, if things went poorly, to hide

his whole army in the Thicket. Collins figured
his boys could hide from Confederate Texas just as good.

Kaiser's men and the militia boys
with Bullock came from towns,
or from the smooth farms of the better counties.
They weren't good for much, or their horses either,
in country that could turn into a pure weather
of yaupon and vines, a brierstorm
with snakes for lightning.
So after stumbling around in there half lost
with wrong-way creeks and the bad heat,
Bullock decided to make use of a dry summer.
He set a circling fire.

Like most people doing anything, the men
who torched it left one hole in the wrong direction
and right there was where Collins' boys tore out,
beside the running deer and varmints, straight through
the open end of a flaming horseshoe and on home
where they sat down to breakfast like anybody would.
Bullock followed with his men, and there was shooting,
and nobody knows exactly why no man was hit
on either fighting side. The army ended up
with nothing to show but one old man named Lilly
shot dead through the suspenders to the heart,
and him no sympathizer to anybody, being afoot
behind an oxteam on the road, coming to pick up
a new cart. A war will do strange things
even off to the side. But fire is predictable,
and this one ate three thousand acres before it quit.
The whole business went so bad that both the captains
went on back to their war and forgot about Collinses.

And their war was over the next year,
nothing changing much one way or the other
here, though more people came to the rest of Texas
from bigger burnouts farther off.
Charlie Bullock stayed alive to get back home,
and Warren Collins stayed glad he hadn't gone
anywhere at all. After awhile, the two of them

17

took to going out hunting together,
firesetter and runner, two old men
and both sides of a story
looking across a campfire at each other
while a pack of hounds mouthed glory after
fox or wolf, and the Thicket closing in
every place but one.

Oil

First Sour Lake, then Saratoga, then Batson
boomed. By 1905, most of the four-legged
wildcats in the Thicket had been scared
at least once by the other kind.
Panthers got tired of having to move their dens.
The smell of sulphur and the tarry air
that had always hovered kind of familiar
over a few bubbling sloughs
was suddenly everywhere as the underneath
cracked open. Sludge, black scum, and spewed-up
salt water crawled over pastures and ruined the creeks.
Oil riggers flared the gas all night to keep it
from blowing up. That much light
spooked woods-ranging livestock clean off
and drove the wild game out.

Not that it wasn't hard on all those people
come from damn near everywhere to find
that getting rich meant getting godforsaken
miserable in mud that could sink a whole wagon
and bog a ten-ox team up to the shoulders,
maybe for days. It was hell trying
to get machinery in there, and hell living
in a tent on ground that never dried all winter.
Outside one boomtown, somebody built a railroad
straight into deep thicket to the wells.
When the boom died out, those same men
took up the tracks and left with the whole thing.

It was as if some awful steady, enormous beast
had got born, lived regular awhile,
then vanished trackless as a dinosaur.

At Batson—after what would become
the Paraffine Oil Company had paid the sum
of eighty thousand dollars into the held-out apron
of the wife of one old landowner who couldn't count—
the world turned over: canvas hotels, open-air saloons,
whorehouses, the usual things that rise
when the money's under something else.
But there were some who'd lived in these woods so long
they didn't know they didn't own the land,
and they developed a deep-set opinion
against people poking holes in it for any reason.

The only way the riggers could get in
or out of the Thicket was on horseback
single file, and even that was hard.
One time, when a worn-out crew came off the derricks
and headed to where they'd tied the transportation,
they found their horses seriously changed.
Upset nesters had got themselves some paint,
every kind of color they could find.
Maybe the riggers thought a vengeful dream
had come for them out of the awful ground
when they saw those horses shining in the sun,
wet, some of them striped, every way looking wrong.
And worse, damned near too jumpy to ride home.

If you could call Batson exactly home,
tent carnival smeared with the black smell of oil,
riches so new there hadn't been lumber cut
to build anything quite real, the jail
a couple of big trees where prisoners were chained;
and people spilling from Ireland, New York, England,
jumped-ship sailors next to out-of-work cowboys,
speculators, thieves, peddlers, swindlers, killers,
living too close together in a haze of sulphur.

Around all that, the Thicket sweated,

19

breathing in and breathing out
paraffin mire, thorns, snakes, sweet cash, and a few
stray puzzled deer right onto main street
where even the idea of oil was new, though the stuff
had once been bottled from the seeps
by a half-Indian who went by the name of Doctor Mud
and wore a top hat, claiming miracles.

Now here in a twilight of owls and Ivory-bills
came twenty horses passing strange,
bright cayuses of Apocalypse, a string of fevers—
greased, half-crazy, cut-loose carousel
    blue   yellow   orange   barn-red
with mad roustabout riders not able to guess
which way they'd be changed themselves
when the whole shebang pulled out for good,
brass-ring rich, wounded, broke, cured, or dead.

Stories, 1940s

For example, Oscar Sawyer's store.
Out front the lone gas pump was red,
the kind already long past use,
a skinny sentry with a head of glass.
The store itself listened toward the road,
leaning by inches in the direction of news
without much more forward margin.

I don't have to tell you how old men
sat outside on wooden drink-crates in good weather,
how they watched. A boy might come by with a pup
or a sack of pecans to sell or trade.
You know what was on the shelves inside:
potted meat, sardines and crackers, rusty traps,
glass candy-jar clouded with sugar dust.

A mile or two back of the store,
Indian village and Spanish mission
slept together two centuries under

Jenkins' farm. That far down, the bones
of the Ays and the priests exchanged conversions,
heat-shimmer on green ears of corn.

Hosey Lucas was always there at Oscar's.
He looked like a man made out of parched cornhusks.
People said that. People waited in the lull
when no car was passing. They knew he'd tell
again how he happened to have that sunk-in place
right in the middle of his forehead—
kicked by a mule when he was twelve
and the whole thing just healed over
without a doctor. Left him potholed
deep enough to set a teacup in,
and he still had good sense.

He might tell about the coon that jumped
straight out of a tree onto Garsee Johnson's back
and rode him home.
Or about the time old man Burton found a track
in the dirt road by his house and thought a snake
that didn't ever wiggle must have made it,
so he got his gun and trailed the thing for miles.
Came up on a bicycle rider resting in the shade.
The old man, who'd never seen a town,
stayed mad a week.
Hosey Lucas and his dog would sit.
And both of them could talk.

Behind them, all the corn could do,
it did—telling long bones, dead fires,
arrows to the sun, the deepening ceremonies
in a new translation.

In far-off places, the future's story began again,
SS gun butts breaking children's heads
completely, the small animals of some woods
unable to live, or even to run in the human heart.
At Los Alamos, people started taking things apart.
Fireflies would spark up early at Oscar's.
Somebody'd say fox hunting had got harder,

21

like you couldn't hear the dogs as good.
And somebody'd come back with, "You just too old
to hear, period."
The dam that in twenty years would take their land
was edging toward a drawing board,
that phantom water
already muting the fox's plume
and muffling the hounds' high laughter.

These dirt farmers would die soon
in their beds, or fall down in a barn.
The red dust wouldn't notice that they'd joined.
Not so you could tell it,
though there might be some kind of difference in the form
that dances in dust-devil wind. If we could see it.
People then could still die in one place,
in the illusion of one piece
of time, and take a wholeness with them into earth
the way an apple does, fallen in tall grass,
unnoticed until nothing's left above ground
except the story, *apple*,
bitter or sweet or poisoned as the real,
and ready for reenactment in the round.

Everything was quiet but the bugs
at Oscar's, nobody talking one August afternoon
when the field of black-eyed susans across the road
took on an extra layer of the light,
a thickening like before a cyclone. And not like that.
Things went dry as a sermon, too still,
as if the air had emptied its glass bottle
just for a minute. Then somebody opened a knife
and peeled a green stick, one long curl
with the sound it makes: a whisper, then a *tick*.
And cleft Hosey Lucas leaned back, mentioning the world.

Photograph of the Courthouse Square, 1950s

Here is the town with its spine broken,
a cough in the dust just risen
behind that Buick's disappearing tail fins.
Dust smears the plate-glass reflections
of farmers on their way to insurance.
Beyond the white borders of this picture,
thick cotton fields are unraveling fast.

You can see it's a Saturday, spit-shiny
sidewalks are crowded. Barge-bosomed women
are taking on cargo, gossip, the strategy
for a new onslaught of gentility.
Only July or August could make the light
this mean. The camera has caught the heat,
how it can shut like a box,
like the click of a dull knife,
holding everything still.

Two children have climbed to the stone knee
of James Pinckney Henderson,
who sits in his stone lawyer's chair on a rock
left rough as Houston's Texas Republic.
Under the pecan tree by the statue,
the men stall in a knot, a quarrel,
a guffaw, a lie. They are forgiving
the wrong politicians again.

There is still one pair of mules hitched
to a wagon in this picture.

In their beaten hats, old men are leaning
toward just this stopped grainy air,
this fading of detail on a piece of paper:
the handwritten deed naming *a pin oak tree*
as permanent west corner of a farm in 1840,
county tax records that disappeared,
bad debts set afire, the birth date changed,
bogus land certificates, crooked leases,
court records vanished after a murder,
indictments misplaced, feuds unreported in print—

paper and its untrustworthy statements.

And most of those in this photograph dead
who knew the world a condition of memory
tenacious as spidersilk, sticky as fear,
its breath the intractable word
I have come for.

II

Remembering Brushing My Grandmother's Hair

I see her in a ring of sewing, light
fingers on needle and hoop, elaborate
scissors shaped like a tiny stork,
the glass egg in her lap.
Her temperate mourning wore black shoes.

Released, her hair released a scent
as I imagined of ascending birds, or smoke
from a burning without source, but cool
as mist over a real country, altars in the hills.
That gray reached all the way to the floor.

A cloak, wind in a cloak, her hair
in my hands crackled and flew. I dreamed her
young and flying from some tallest room
before she had to let her power down
for something to take hold and climb.

Permanence. Rose and vine were twisted
hard in silver on the brush and mirror.
Above us, the accurate clock pinged:
always on a time there comes a sleep
stony as a tower, with the wild world beneath,

and wound like this with locked bloom tarnishing—
I brushed. She sewed or dozed. The child I was
stood shoulder-deep in dying, in a dress of falling
silver smoothed by silver, a forgetfulness
dimming the trees outside the window like a rain.

To grow to stay, to braid and bend
from one high window—
I guessed the story I would learn by heart:
how women's hands among sharp instruments
learn sleep, the frieze like metal darkening,
the land sown deep with salt.

Exchange

In the cavernous, tin-ceilinged back room
of THE FARMER'S EXCHANGE, GENERAL MERCHANDISE,
cloth sacks of flour were piled in a mountain
shedding constant snow, powdering a weave of its own
on the stacked extra harnesses, bullwhips, boxes
of boots, nail barrels, dead cockroaches,
and the flypaper hanging in useless loops.

Saturdays we sneaked there to ruin
all credible arrangement, to burn up
in a white summer of dreams while the working
sun edged in the back door from the alley,
slow as another customer with no money.

Hefting walls of our future bread
into castles and forts, we leaped over
to land in original tracks, explorers.
We knew the movies, a few books, school-yard sex—
everything in the world that we knew
was usable. Once I dropped a lit cigarette
between slats of a crate, and we couldn't get to it.
All that night in our beds awake,
we kept a pact of prayer against fire,
against sirens that could unzip the dark,
everything that we knew in the world
its flammable secret.

We wrote notes in code, left them rolled
in the empty throats of pop bottles
crated to go, addressed to kindred souls
surely trapped at the far end of Coca-Cola's line,
forced there to wash and refill maybe a million,
and waiting for rescue only we could arrange.
Whatever was beyond changing waited for us.

Through the arch between storeroom and trade,
we could just see our mothers and fathers
still talking up front. And they paled
in the white breath made of our motion.
We could let them go on fading forever
in the storm we had hung on the air.
Or we could come forth and forgive them
back to the living.

Found, dragged home to be scolded,
we left our ghost step on the sidewalk.
Probably somebody would have to pay
for a bag of flour broken,
and always we would have to say we were sorry
and be looked at, bad children
bleached as biscuits, encoded as spirits,
shaking our real hair out of a cloud.

Were we not beautiful then?—miller's daughters
able to spin and be counted, warriors,
discoverers willing to get there in time,
ourselves the gold coming through.

The Kinds of Sleep

First there's the one in which all the children
your parents wanted you to be are chosen.
The sheep from the goats they said in Sunday school.
You remember judgment: it's cool as blue marble,
quiet as a hospital. All the others
have been led to honeyed pastures—
is that it? Anyhow, you are the only goat,
stuck in a stone place with your own sad smell.
Nobody cares if you wake up.

You may sleep to believe in ink.
It seems to be ink but there's more of it,
viscid, a blot that will cover everything.
And with no words in it, nothing but black.
You have been made responsible. So you push,
you push to save whatever you can from the dark.
It seeps through your fingers, gets worse.
For a whole mysterious night you have to be Sisyphus
lacking a stone, wrestling an angel of pitch,
the black in *black plague*, the perfect
coherence of floodwaters.
You give your right arm for an edge.

Then there's the walking sleep.
It's dark, but somehow the right house
assembles itself under your feet.
You step into air and it's there,
the kitchen with the pie-safe and pictures
of white roosters, the dining room window
framing oak trees and the fishpond;
the rooms with their sentinel fireplaces
coming to be in your footfall.
A thorntree of fear grows in your throat
when you remember the house
will end, used up, at the porch rail
beyond which the rest of your life
is creating you step by step.

Last is the sleep with flowers
and the golden fishes you have come to feed,
a child with raw oatmeal in your pocket,

zinnias in your leftover Easter basket.
This is the sweet one. You have forgotten
everything except morning where it is always morning,
and your ignorance surrounding you with green,
with presence, with your body that can merge,
like the pomegranate on its tree by the fence,
with light. All that you never want to know
has gone, has not come. You slip off the last
porch step into the dewy grass, the path
to the pool where goldfish break black water
that folds again into night above their lanterns.
The goat in the pasture lends you his eye of surprise
as the world fails and you step onto white
   bedsheet   feathers   paper   snow
on which you will lie down, not even flailing
an angel shape, not breathing your small tune, not
writing your name.

Woman in a Series of Photographs

Cold mornings, one foot
touching an icy floor, the bare
tree framed unchanging
like a crack in the windowpane.

Out of the cold of those mornings,
the stone at my mother's head
tightened around me, air
that could only ask me to be still.

Still, here was the way I dried my hair in summer,
spread out on a quilt in the grass,
the warm world, the yellow.
That was my father's season.

Between the two of them I was taught
everything, doubling, how the mirror
loves, then lets me slip out with the dark.
Half of the world is always invisible.

In that porch swing all July
I read a book about galleons.
Wasn't I a tall ship getting ready
good-bye to the quilt's yellow patch,
to the grass that would sear where I sailed?

But that was all invention.
The way my eyes dreamed was always
the way windows are veiled
in tight rooms when winter's fires are lit.

In my heart I was somebody quick.
In the house, in the yard, a stone.
It wasn't bad—that way I had of looking
without seeming to pay attention.
I saw more than a bargain.

Now I am fifty I see how to grow
alone is a blessing that gets bigger
to accommodate the necessary.
I am wearing a yellow dress

you can't see. That is one way to be
joyful. All the deaths
ahead of me I remember already.

And this bare black tree, fissure
around which such clarity is grasped.

Rent House

I can't think why I've come to see this
house with no resonance, temporary
years between the real houses: that one
I was born to, the other I traveled from.
The interim is here, habitual, stupefied
summers of brass and blue enamel,
smudged backyard grass of fall.
Everything that was here still
stands except the cannas. The journey
of the same cracked two-strip driveway
ends the same.

Before this, the short life it feels like dreaming
to remember: field and barn, pecan trees,
the rambling gentle house holding its own
wide skirts of pasture, fluttering henyard,
and my live mother close.
The town doctor's had that place for thirty years,
all the pecans, sunset behind the fence rail,
a bed of asters in the filled-in fish pool.

The last of childhood left me in yet another
house, five unsteady porches, grandparents,
a spread wing floating me along until I simmered
into leaving.
Years ago, a retired contractor from Houston
restored that one to unremembered splendor.

This narrow house between.
I look a long time, thinking
I need imagination, but there's nothing
to be made of such temporal defeat.
How long was it we lived on this back street
behind screens billowing with rust?
I remember how long one afternoon
I wrote my whole name broad and hard in crayon
on every single windowscreen in this house,
and then was punished.
Forsythia is the name of those flowers
I watched darken in the wallpaper.

All night I'd listen to the child next door
cry and cut teeth. Now he's a lawyer
in San Francisco. I matched his howls
with those I kept back. Both our voices
ran down the moony street alongside crossed
adult allegiances that roamed, like ghostly wolves,
the nights of any town so old.

Nobody rented in a town like this.
Why did papa bring me here
to this aunt who makes me braid my hair?
Where is my mother?
Where's the calf you said was mine?
What happened to the trees?
Then they'd drive me out there so I'd see
fields dizzy with briers, the derelict house
large and sad and creatureless.
Until I lost even my loss, got used
to a cramped hallway and a makeshift life,
the tight backyard with no hen in it.

And it was here I staked a claim: from any room
I could look up to see my name
purple or lime green against the sun,
or clearer, lamplit on the night outside.
Nothing they tried would get it off
those years I thinned down, toughening,
asthmatic with grief and discovery:
how the self, amazed, swam up like bone
through the lost landscape, through the mother's
vanished flesh, through all remembered
and all future home,
to build garish letters on the riddled air,
knowing there's no place else. Not anywhere.

Plath

I

Aurelia, your child had a talent
for beautiful hatreds.
She grew them like tulips, all red.
She grew them like moons in a system
of mirrors, gibbous children,
perfection of tubers and pallors.

She took the world for a room
of her own. A bit like a tomb.
Or the inside of a bomb.
It was done so exceptionally well,
not even the weather could tell:
the trees gone obediently bald,
the clouds like an executioner's wall
speaking her language out loud.

She could bloody a universe in her thumb.

Medusa, she translated you.
But that was her likeness, all serpenty hair
in the looking glass fastened with hook and screw
onto hills, and the sea, other people, the air—
dead ringers, dead ringers everywhere
she looked. There was nothing, nothing to do
but turn into stone after brilliant stone.

A whole cemetery of *one*.

II

I am ashamed of this anger, ashamed
that I can no longer feel sorry for her,
the American girl who made herself over,
made herself an Auschwitz to fit,
cobbling, cobbling the black shoe
until she could marry it, marry it.

Ambitious as metal or jewels,
that fury reflects, refracts
beyond the reach of academic necrophiliacs,
the puffing of suicide buffs,

36

the industry and swagger of sexual
politicians male and female.
Such poetry cannot be unfaithful.
It stands like one of those reptiles
dead for millennia,
skeletal track of a tranced
imperative engine—
bone-castle so massive and glittery
no future could ever have lived in it,
neither art's nor woman's.

III

Aurelia, it is you I would listen for
in the long-willed silence.
Mentioned only because of the letters
(those voices of wire and saccharin)
a footnote in the interpreters' jargon,
you were the mother of death, who had to bear it.

I imagine you beside me at the supermarket
in practical shoes, a plaid coat;
an ordinary woman whose pain was not usable,
any ordinary woman alive
whispering the price of fruit.

There is no metaphor for it.

Corner of Pawnee and Broadway

Canst thou bind the unicorn
with his band in the furrow?
— Job 39:10

Beached on a Wichita street corner
by three-dollar wheat, drought, and the general wind,
he wore the inevitable wide-brimmed hat
hiding his eyes that anyway would tell us
nothing.
　　　　He stood beside a harvest that would sell,
paintings-on-velvet brought from Texas by the gross:
Rambo full-length, deft, akimbo with weapons
against a softened night,
John Wayne close up, squint and jawful of heft.
Last, and lined up straighter than the rest,
sweet-faced unicorns, white as Christmas,
on a dime-store sparkle of planetary dark.

"I used to be a wheat farmer," he said.
"Three-quarters of my sales is unicorns.
I don't know what that means."
We hadn't asked. We left him looking weathered
as driftwood in a phosphorescence
of raised fists, Saturday-cartoon desire
glittering on the spiral horn no creature
but the narwhal ever wore.

Corpse-whale. Sailors in the Middle Ages
thought it augured shipwreck.
And they risked it, bringing back the ornament
merchants would sell by inches to the richest
terrors of the time; and set in gold to dress St. Mark's.
It passed for proof against poison, solar zenith,
virgin lure—and into holiness:
the horn not a horn, the unicorn not
even approximately the hiding real
neutral beast of the neutral sea,
spinning its peaceful courtship emblem
long and long in the meadows of the ice.

The plains wind laps at ruin. Less and less
can stick to the tacky nap of grief
out here where farms fall into dark as if
the Kansas sky had flung
its twisting harpoons everywhere at once.
And all the stories get each other wrong.

The stories always get each other wrong,
though something works in every missed connection,
every failed mystery, even on velvet, even from Texas.
One day we saw the prairie air take on
such density as only water has, or desperation,
and people go on moving in that depth,
working, glancing at the sky, buying for hope
the image of leviathan's sweetened tooth.

Digression on the Nuclear Age

In some difficult part of Africa, a termite tribe
builds elaborate tenements that might be called
cathedrals, were they for anything so terminal
as Milton's God. Who was it said
the perfect arch will always separate
the civilized from the not? Never mind.
These creatures are quite blind and soft
and hard at labor chemically induced.
Beginning with a dish-like hollow, groups
of workers pile up earthen pellets.
A few such piles will reach a certain height;
fewer still, a just proximity.
That's when direction changes, or a change
directs: the correct two bands of laborers
will make their towers bow toward each other.
Like saved and savior, they will meet in air.
It is unambiguously an arch and it will serve,
among the others rising and the waste,
an arch's purposes. Experts are sure
a specific moment comes when the very structure
triggers the response that will perfect it.

I've got this far and don't know what
termites can be made to mean. Or this poem:
a joke, a play on arrogance, nothing
but language? Untranslated, the world gets on
with dark, flawless constructions rising,
rising even where we think we are. And think
how we must hope convergences will fail this time,
that whatever it is we're working on won't work.

Pasture Burn-off at Midnight

*"I think it kind of fascinated them," farmer Robert Brown
said. "A lot of cattle have never seen fire. People just don't
think about things like that."*

—newspaper caption
with color photograph
Wichita *Eagle-Beacon*

Bad weather grass so poor nothing would eat it
but this: deliberate, standing in rows
like smaller red-wavering silos—
whuff and bellow, this bends
to lie spreading, upstumbling
in gust and dry hiss.
Out of shadow the cattle move edgily
close to a grazing brightness.

Not threatened, though every coarse hair
is raised on their shoulders, they stand
in their daytime way. And a morning
comes to their foreheads
where no god's eye is, nor ours
to see red. No stolen ochre can lie
on this field the spectrum has never
unfolded, where the story
without us is told.

Here, light in its plainest guise
walks like a risen river,
original lifting of darkness,
stark simple, unstabled.

Black-eyed as icons, the cattle
are gathered in the eternal
ceremony of wind. All their lives
the invisible breathing of prairies
has moved in every intensity on them.
Now something has married that motion,
eating the field dust and grass
to become a creaturely dancing

beheld,
>   and the cattle are tranced in it.
Rib cages rocking like arks
they are borne in a kinship from dark.

Flat-eyed and taken, bereft
of the colors of history,
they have seen
in slowed-down animal time
the wind's one countenance as light
in its once-only coming to pass
that shall not be ours—
whose darkness grew deeper than night,
whose radiance was changed while we slept.

But see how the cattle are watching
the wind-voice and touch of the world
take hold. Until what has sheerly danced
for them will lie down in their faith
as ordinary sun greening fields
that could save even us in the sightless
comb of bright air. And the ashes
blowing every which way.

On the Way to Write a Poem in the 1980s

At first it will be like one of those maps
for tourists, but with everything missing:
world blank as windless ocean except
for the one small square, like a raft,
inexplicably marked *you are here*.

Spinner, spinnaker, spindrift,
made of the stuff you're lost in,
you have to throw out your life,
thread of bailwater,
stuttering groundline, thin note
bodiless with hope.

You can't stay becalmed in the mirror,
or rock in the psychiatric tremor,
trick out a broken net
for theory (our late-century ur-story
of world that always gets away).
You have to get past loose ironies
with hooks in them, and all that conversation,
the surfaces suburban as a lawn.

You are the knot untied but still trying
again with the real tears, memory's interior
silks outflung:
water spelling the world in the palm
of the deaf-mute child,
letter by letter. Or *world*
that wrote itself on the hand of water.
Either one of these you'll take on faith.
Or both.

The high white cross
against the sky holds fast its heron,
the dark stoop its hawk
over fields where the noon-stunned cow
and the grasshopper and mouse are spoken,
wild asters and the far house
you'll take for home.

And here you will have caught
ruins entirely outside the guidebooks
no matter how deftly shuffled or wisely dealt:
the skyward glint of warhead-bearing planes,
and swells of more than old seas underground
where silos tilt toward shipwreck,
the whole coded boneyard in their holds.

It goes this far. It goes all the way.
Landfall seeps from the horizon, becomes
itself—and this map
like a spider's wake aglitter:
world hangs in its fingers
clear as that moment when,
between two lovers, a sorrow
spoken places them forever—
the one embrace just broken. *Now
you are here.*

The Case for Gravity

Hydrangeas bloomed beside the house,
globes of blue light blurring in the rain
that finally broke the gold, hot pane of summer
that summer I was five.
I leaned from the high porch-edge over a sea
that spread, sudden as creation's, in the flower bed.
All afternoon beneath the unclenched sky
our tin roof sang small change.

And the drenched oak had dropped a few
mutable leaves. Five-finned they floated,
multiplying as if the wind
meant something new.
I reached with a bent pin on a string,
fishing until I leaned too far and lost
my hold on the house. Time turned then
all space, all bright blue slow drift

of planets sheared entirely loose for one
stopped second when it seemed I flew
or swam in nothing. And the nothing swam.
I flopped hard, like a trout,
on a world gone bust, blue bits of it
floating sweetly down the pewter air
as I stood up baptized with mud,
a pain like bands of bells around my head,
blood in my eyes.

After the first fall, there are the others:
vertigo's possibilities, the love
like a dropped cup, all hope
spilled so out of reach the world lets go
to bluest distance.
                    Always the ground
reels me in to its cruel flowers, nothing ideal,
blue taste of beauty on the bitten tongue.
Say this time too I'll stand
mud-colored, abloom with bruises, vivid with news.

Say these are sheaves of fishes in my hands.

III

Cape Sounion

This light is never silent,
washing the rocks with loud blue,
clamoring in wild flowers—
tocsin of blood-red poppies,
sanctus of *peruka* and *narkissos*.
It hides a lyre in the shaken temple
whose marble sings false white
to every boat.
Seen close, the stone is harsh,
hoarding the gold of deserts and their lions
in the long throats of the columns.

Words. Here are the travelers: English,
German, Italian—the dates of our centuries
scratched on the pillars. Byron's name
struck high and silly.
Nothing we've attached dulls the assault
or contains it. Or can make open
any door to leak us whole
through this aurorean rumble.

It's sheer luck, our being here
alone—no picnickers, no tourist buses—
with the old salt god and our inadequate praises,
and the whole day falling clangorous down the sky.
We've pocketed the useless,
music we remember, change, sunglasses.

A broken relief too poor for the museums
leans against a foundation. It shimmers
and thrums in the beaten grass: half a horse,
its one eye gone, mane barely preserving the wind
and the panic. One foreleg is raised terribly
against the drone of loss.

The image has caught us
as if a net went out from it
woven entirely of rift.
If we listen, we will be taken
and partial forever, given half
to rubble and grass, the rest

a bronze note struck with such force
all outline
will be driven back into stone,
defeated form humming under the skin.

If we listen.

Only the merciless light
rides a whole horse on these mountains.

Cycladic

I

Every pale American April my eyes will ache
with stolen blue, and the Greek sky become
more real than this one. The cracked icon
of rock will rise in its robe of salt
from that wind-dazzled sea, the island
breaking among its broken legends,
dove-winging out of time, wearing the chain
of whitened villages—so purely
world I want to marry this, to wake again
in the swayed bed with its pillow of raw wool,
smell of sheep oil and ashes.

Our house with its tilted portraits
of Andreas' fisher grandfathers, the kitchen
and little shrine, wallholder of plastic flowers,
the garden of artichokes—from the terrace,
surrounded with tossing fretful roses,
we could see all the way to Paros,
stepped fields dropping away to the sea
like a traveler's tale, and the winds
of the high farm rearranging
our notions of music around our ears.

Downward toward death we found this,
late when our losses were blooming around us
bright as *paparouna* that stained the feet
of the olive trees. Blood of Adonis become
Christ's blood by the simple miracle of time,
those poppies reddened every unstirred field,
every lopped vineyard, remembering
all the stories.

The villagers have shut away meat and oil
as if only hunger can remind the soul.

Now the women are whitewashing the houses,
the stairs in the wall, even the mortar
between the drunken stones of the street.
The priest has blessed the sheep with *vaya*.
Boiled wheat and the pomegranate's red coals

51

are laid on the graves to warm the dead.
With a church of blossom on their shoulders,
the villagers have borne the *Epitaphios*,
bier of violets, lemon flowers, roses
for the flat-eyed dark wood mountain Christ.

II

And we said the whole island existed
only for cleansing and baking, for the old men
and the grandmothers waiting; that there come
again the one true midnight of the year,
an Easter with its ancient heart of fire
spilling from every blue-doored church
into the mazy streets
a racket to raze the black dome of heaven:
rockets, gunshots, and half a hundred
suddenly unwidowed bells run mad
across the night-backed mountains.

Then is the donkey risen
from his long straw dream, speaking
the names of God in the ragged language of donkeys.
The wronged cock's crow and the goat's slant hymn
are risen, floating over the star-flecked bay
that sings like a thresher in its broken circle.
Young birds in the churchyards,
startled out of their nests
by the blinding hard holy noise,
are ground underfoot by the pious.

Now they can walk with their desire
toward the oiled meat and resined wine,
toward the dance that waits spitted
on strings of violin and *laouto*.
Village to bell-shaken village
the procession moves, tearing open
the egg of the darkness.
They have made it release its promise
in candlefire streaming over the shoulders
of every fisherman and kerchiefed girl,

every widow and farmer and saint-struck child.
Even the months-old baby wears the gilded kiss
of the icon on his mouth alight,
alight in the narrow street.

Already Yannis warms his battered violin
in the taverna's fragrance of *mayeritsa*.
He has tucked a daisy behind his ear.
At any moment he may take root,
a night-blooming song with a day's eye,
dark quarter tones unfolding their petals,
shading toward dawn.
Yannis the butcher plays, flowers,
sings, and flows like the wine.
The people will dance until they fall down.

III

Remember, love, how the village woke late
in a wash of sun that stung like new *retsina*
from Nikos' barrel? Now the animals
drowse in their walled fields to forget
the night's uncommon rousing.
As the sea sleeps in its shawl of nets,
forgetting the draught of stars.

Christos anesti. Alithos anesti.
In all the houses, they rub sore eyes and stand.
Old Eleni from the highest village
wears many skirts on her way to the harbor,
her eyes on the bay as it rises to meet her.
Another day the boat will come to disgorge
rolls of wire, news, cases of yogurt,
boiling black motorcycles.
But today there are no arrivals.
The sea is an aged face full of heaven
wrinkled with mild wind.
Bearing baskets of sweetened bread for her cousins,
and a lament in her throat, Eleni walks
with all her names wild in the air around her.
When she smiles, the goddesses of stone

are disarmed, and the icons are emptied of women.
Many times she has given and taken Him.
Her mouth is slick with fat.

Crowlike in the coat he wears for plowing,
Andreas had milked his three goats.
He sits on the low wall to rest his swollen knees.
Beside him, the bucket of bright blue plastic
steams like a tiny engine.
For his wife he has stored in his pocket
sprigs of *righani*, herb whose name means
mountain brightness, whose flavor
awakens the meat.
Sometimes, when the taverna's music is sharp
as cut garlic, he remembers to sing
the verses belonging only to this island,
love and death; and his voice
will clothe him anew in darkness,
centuries of dead sons,
war after war, the long names
bitter on his tongue.

IV

Among red eggshells and the blackened ends
of candles saved for their holy power
to quieten storms, the shadows
knife toward noon.
Every olive tree clinging to the mountain
is feathered in its own metallic light.
The terraced fields begin to remember their wheat.
And on the highest, almost inaccessible peak,
the abandoned monastery of Profitis Elias
gives back to Helios his white fire.

We made our procession.
It walks in us, footsteps of stone
lightened to fragrance of almond and rosemary
trailing the sea like a skirt.
We cannot lose this anywhere,

last birthplace, schist and dry ground,
sweet loaf, bitter wine, fig tree, dovecote.

It turns up
in the white pebble I keep on a shelf,
in any speech of water, in the tamed red
of the potted geranium, the scent of the herb jar.
Come round like a scythe edge,
this boat made of rock and blossom
arrives on time on its own
goat-footed wind,
the next note of Yannis' crooked song
out of the blue.